Let *Justice* Roll Down

Women Engaging the World

Rebecca Seiling

Faith & Life Resources
A division of Mennonite Publishing Network
Mennonite Church USA and
Mennonite Church Canada

Harrisonburg, Virginia
Waterloo, Ontario

Let Justice Roll Down
Women Engaging the World
Copyright © 2012 by Faith & Life Resources, Harrisonburg, Virginia 22802
             Released simultaneously in Canada by Faith & Life Resources,
             Waterloo, Ontario N2L 6H7. All rights reserved.
International Standard Book Number: 978-0-8361-9624-5
Printed in United States of America
Cover design by Merrill Miller, design by Mary Meyer
Cover photo by Jaroslav/iStockphoto/Thinkstock

Unless otherwise noted, Scripture text is quoted, with permission, from the *New Revised Standard Version*, © 1989, Division of Christian Education of the National Council of Churches of Christ in the United States of America.

Hymns referenced in this book are from *Hymnal: A Worship Book* (Faith & Life Resources, 1992), *Sing the Journey* (Faith & Life Resources, 2005), and *Sing the Story* (Faith & Life Resources, 2007).

The content for this book was sponsored jointly by Mennonite Women USA and Mennonite Women Canada.

To order or request information, please call 1-800-245-7894 in the U.S. or 1-800-631-6535 in Canada. Or visit www.faithandliferesources.org.

16 15 14 13 12 11 10   10 9 8 7 6 5 4 3 2 1

Contents

Preface

L et justice roll down like a mighty river and righteousness like an ever-flowing stream. —Amos 5:24

What a beautiful image: a powerful torrent of justice and righteousness! Our world is filled with stories of courageous people who strive for a world of peace. At the same time, there are countless examples of people yearning for God's reign to come.

This Bible study guide examines the book of Amos and his call to the Israelite people. Over the course of 13 sessions, we will dive into Amos's words and wonder together about their application to us today. To aid in the study, there is a map on page 63 of the Northern and Southern Kingdoms in Amos's time.

As I read Amos, the similarities between Israel then and North America today struck me. Amos the prophet spoke to the wealthy, those who had become complacent. They worshiped God at the temple but neglected the poor among them. Amos does not mince words; he calls the people to change their ways to avoid God's judgment. His message challenged the way that I imagine God, and pushed me to consider a God who "roars" at injustice.

"I want justice!" you might hear someone say. What does justice mean? Other words to describe this broad term include compromise, fairness, accountability, restoration, closure, equality, freedom, setting things right, restitution, peace, compensation, reconciliation, and even revenge. In the Bible, there is a close connection between the words "justice" and "righteousness." This guide will look at several arenas where justice can be served—from the home, to the church community, to international economic policies.

The prophet's role is to speak God's word into a situation. In Walter Brueggemann's *The Prophetic Imagination,* he writes, "It is the vocation of the prophet to keep alive the ministry of imagination, to keep on conjuring and proposing futures alternative to the single one the king wants to urge as the only thinkable one" (p. 40).

As women in North America, we are called to lives of justice. Amos's urgent pleas and petitions to those who are "at ease" and living comfortable lives are needed today, just as they were thousands of years ago.

I invite you to join me on this exploration of the book of Amos. I'll warn you: it is not for the faint of heart. Amos shakes, disturbs, and pushes our comfort zones. If you are content with the life you're living, do not read Amos. It is dangerous, challenging reading. If we follow Amos's example, we will speak out against the injustices in our time, listen to an outsider's critiques, confront the powers that be, and become ministers of imagination—imagining and working toward a new world that is aligned with God's purposes.

Strength and grace be with you as you engage in this study of Amos.

Rebecca Seiling
Waterloo, Ontario

A Word on the Use of This Guide

Spiritual growth involves learning to know God through the Scriptures and through life experience. Thus, the sessions in this guide begin with a scriptural overview and move to personal experience through the visuals and thoughts of the gathering time. The "Deepening" part of each session returns to reflection on Scripture, and is followed by integrating questions that relate the session to our own lives. The closing brings together both scriptural insights and life-lessons in an atmosphere of prayer.

Women can use this guide in a variety of ways.

1 . Both individual reflection and/or group sharing. Women read the lessons during the week, or at the beginning of the session, and choose one or two questions to ponder. In a group setting, each participant might then share her thoughts and insights with the others. This approach recognizes that group sharing is deeply enriched through time for personal reflection. The role of the leader is to facilitate sharing rather than to "teach" the lessons. The leader will need to focus on one or two questions rather than trying to include them all.

2 . A more traditional approach. The makeup of your group is essential to the format you choose as leader. A teaching group is more likely to emphasize the "Deepening" section than the integrating questions, which are quite personal in nature. Here are a few questions that you as a leader might use in order to promote interaction with the material presented in the "Deepening" section:

- How have you understood this passage in the past?

- What is new or different about the ideas presented here?

- What do you find interesting or intriguing?

- What makes you uncomfortable?

- What feelings do you notice as you reflect on this session?

- How might the Spirit be inviting you to grow?

3 . Shorter meditations. The group or individual might want to use only the overview, visuals, and gathering for shorter meditations. A more elderly group, for example, may not be inclined to ask the deeper, probing questions. They might be very responsive, however, to sharing stories and memories sparked by the section on gathering.

Whatever the makeup of your group, pray for spiritual growth in an atmosphere of trust, confidentiality, and respect. As women of faith, may we grow in confidence and wisdom as we receive our gifts from God and share them with others.

one. . . . .

The Prophetic Voice

READING: Amos 7:10-14

OVERVIEW

Throughout the prophetic books of the Bible, a steady drumbeat can be heard: return to God's ways, remember who you are, seek justice. These calls are persistent, and bring harsh words of coming judgment. Amos, whose name means "burden bearer," carried a heavy, sobering message of warning to Israel.

Amos has two vocations in two very different locations. In Judah, he is a herdsman and a tender of trees, and in Israel, he is a prophet of the Lord. Amos preaches at a time when the Assyrian empire is threatening to advance on Israel from the north. He travels from Tekoa in the Southern Kingdom of Judah to the Northern Kingdom of Israel to bring an unwelcome word of judgment (see map on page 63). As an outsider, Amos announces that the impending invasion will be God's punishment.

VISUAL: construction paper megaphone or long cardboard tube

GATHERING

A voice is something unique to each one of us. Imagine the sound of God's voice. Is it tender and sweet, high or low, raspy or deep? Listen to the sound of your own voice through a megaphone.

Amos introduces us to a God whose voice roars like a lion. He brought God's voice to the people of Israel. Amos was most likely not a popular guest in Israel, but he felt called to leave his herds and groves of trees to speak about God's judgment and hope.

Prophets like Amos often spoke in public settings like the market, the city gate, or in front of the temple. Their messages drew attention; they were pointed, poetic, and memorable. Perhaps Amos started out with an authoritative voice, or maybe his voice was small and grew with intensity.

I have observed street-corner preachers who feel burdened to bring a message to passers-by. As they stand on wooden boxes, their loud voices carry across the sidewalks and seem to fall on deaf ears. Did Amos have a similar reception? Did most people ignore him, or were they engaged and moved to action?

Think about your own experience. When has God called you to speak? When have you spoken up, even when your message was unpopular?

DEEPENING

In Amos 7:10-14, the priest Amaziah complains to King Jeroboam about Amos's conspiracy against Israel. Amos's words must be having quite an impact, because Amaziah declares, "the land is not able to bear all his words." Amaziah even tells Amos to go back to Judah to prophesy.

In the ancient world, words carried immense power. The words themselves had power to bring about change. Spoken blessings and curses were not merely words, but a form of action. In Genesis 1, God spoke and the world was formed.

Prophets held many roles in the Old Testament. Nathan was an advisor to King David, and played a central role in the king's decisions. Amos spoke to the empire from outside the court. We hear of interesting behavior from prophets—wearing uncomfortable clothing (Elijah), wearing a yoke (Jeremiah), and lying down on one side for over a year (Ezekiel). More than anything else, the prophet's role was to engage in politics and speak the word of the Lord into a current situation.

In Amos 3:7-8, Amos declares: "The Lord God has spoken; who can but prophesy?" He seems compelled to speak. In *Living a Life that Matters*, Harold S. Kushner quotes Abraham Joshua Heschel: "To be a prophet is more than an invitation. It is a sense of yielding to overwhelming force against one's will" (p. 94). Kushner sees the prophet's primary role not as one who tells the future, but as one who tells the truth.

Prophets can threaten the status quo. Like society, the church has often rejected prophets out of fear. For countless years, women's voices have also been silenced. But Joel 2:28 reads: "Then afterward I will pour out my spirit on all flesh; your sons *and your daughters* shall prophesy, your old men shall dream dreams, and your young men shall see visions." Women are called to have a prophetic voice today.

In *The Prophetic Imagination*, Walter Brueggemann writes about the community of faith's alternative vision. The church's vocation is to *critique* the dominant culture and to *energize* our communities by providing this vision.

Early Anabaptists took a courageous stand for what they believed God was saying to the church in the 1500s—a stand that sometimes cost their lives. Women held important and prophetic roles in the fledgling Anabaptist churches. Today we carry the same responsibility to critique and energize.

INTEGRATING

1. What prophetic voices have been heard or silenced through the ages? Tell stories of women and men who have criticized and energized the church through their prophetic voices.

2. Amos was keenly aware of current issues. Some church groups have traditionally been the "quiet in the land," keeping to themselves and avoiding matters of the state. Other groups have seen their role toward government as prophetic. How is your church involved politically and why?

3. Amos did not see himself as a prophet, but God called to him, "Go, prophesy to my people Israel." When has your vocation changed based on a call from God? What do you see as your God-given calling?

4. Think about where the prophetic voice is needed in our world today. What message could you give to your community?

CLOSING

Sing "Wild and Lone the Prophet's Voice" (*Sing the Story* #8).

Pray: *God of newness, embolden us to speak your vision to the world around us. Like the prophet Amos, help us to embrace the vocation to which you have called us. Give us your eyes to see the world. Give us your voice to speak your words. Amen.*

Naming the Evils: With Privilege Comes Responsibility

READING: Amos 1–2

OVERVIEW

Amos doesn't waste any time. One by one, he names the neighboring countries and sins they have committed. We can imagine the Israelites nodding in agreement as Amos condemns their enemies for the evils they have done. Then Amos turns the tables. Judah, his home country, has also done evil in God's sight. But the greatest list of sins is saved for Israel.

Amos condemns the nations one by one, getting geographically closer to Judah and Israel (see map on page 63). The noose is tightening. The nations will be judged for crimes against humanity: violence, brutality, slavery, injustice, and revenge. When Amos points to Judah, he accuses the people of rejecting God's covenant laws. And Israel has committed a whole laundry list of wrongs. For the Israelites who were listening, this must have come as quite a shock.

VISUAL: car keys

GATHERING

When I was learning to drive a car, I was aware of what a great responsibility it was. My dad coached me from the passenger seat, trying to impress on me the gravity of this new venture. By not driving properly, he told me, I could take others' lives and even my own. This was a big deal.

Over the years, I had some harder lessons to learn when it came to driving. In my early 20s, I racked up so many speeding tickets that I was summoned to a seminar called "Speed Kills." On another occasion, I got into an accident with another driver.

The privilege of driving comes with a lot of responsibility to myself, my car, pedestrians, animals, and other drivers on the road. Privileges can feel like weighty responsibilities. Amos calls us to consider our privileges as North American women and the accompanying responsibilities.

DEEPENING

Israel's sins don't look as bad as some of the other nations' offenses. But their long list tells us that God is even more disappointed with Israel. They know better. They are not living up to their privileged position as covenant partners with God. Even though Israel, under Jeroboam II, is at the height of its prosperity, Amos delivers a sobering lament. This prosperity has come at the cost of justice.

Many times I've wondered why I was born into a life of relative privilege while others in the world have next to nothing. As North Americans, we have a responsibility to use our wealth wisely. Privilege brings responsibility, and at times this can seem like a heavy load to carry.

Several passages in the New Testament speak of this responsibility. Luke 12:48 states, "From everyone to whom much has been given, much will be required; and from the one to whom much has been entrusted, even more will be demanded." As Christians, we are to take the log out of our own eyes before noticing the speck in someone else's eye (Matthew 7:5).

Sometimes we can also see other churches or denominations in a negative light. Amos pushes us to look at ourselves before critiquing others.

Amos warns Israel of its pride. We can view the crimes of other nations as evil, while neglecting ways that our own country is doing wrong. Sometimes we can also see other churches or denominations in a negative light. Amos pushes us to look at ourselves before critiquing others.

Israel was God's chosen nation, and therefore had a certain status and special responsibilities. The Israelites were expected to keep the covenant law because of this chosen status. How is the church living out its chosen calling? What does this privilege require of us?

INTEGRATING

1. Are there ways that you are not living up to your calling? When could God tell you that "you know better"?

2. Amos is reminding the Israelites of their call to care for the poor. How are we actively concerned for the poor? How are we confronting the evils in our context?

3. At the beginning of Amos, God's voice roars. This is a powerful image. Is it one that inspires you as a woman? Sometimes we may be silent because we, like Israel, stand to benefit from keeping things just the way they are. Does your voice roar because of injustices that you see in our world? What makes God roar today? What would change about your church if you saw yourselves as roaring lions?

4. What charges might Amos bring to your context today?

CLOSING

Sing about being a chosen people:

"God has chosen me" (*Sing the Story* #114)
"Here I am, Lord" (*Hymnal: A Worship Book* #395)
"Beloved, God's chosen" (*Sing the Journey* #38)

Have each woman take out and hold a key or wallet as a symbol of responsibility.

Pray: *God of all good, we are mindful of the ways that you have given us responsibility. Help us to remember you in our actions, big and small. As we use our money and possessions, we remember those who have less. Amen.*

A God Who Roars

READING: Amos 1:2; 3:7-8

OVERVIEW

Between two roars of a lion, Amos pronounces God's judgment on the nations. The image of God portrayed in Amos—one who judges, roars, punishes, and commits acts of unthinkable violence—may not sit well with us.

Our mental pictures of God are important. These images can deeply affect how we treat others and how we see ourselves.

VISUAL: large glass jar

GATHERING

Many of us have ingrained images of God. Some people think of God as a person. Others think of God as a spirit, or as a rock, or wind, or river. Some think of God as a man: a dad who is strong, loving, and deeply compassionate. Others might picture God as a woman: a mom who is warm, hospitable, and generous.

It's hard for me to reconcile these positive images with a God who roars or a God who is about to destroy Israel. "My" God doesn't punish, doesn't use violence, doesn't judge. But am I creating God in my image?

One of the most striking images of God in the Old Testament comes when God appears to Moses in a burning bush. God's self-definition here—"I am who I am," or "I will be who I will be"—is an active definition. It is a verb rather than a noun, and it is open to change.

Usually I'm happy to keep God in a box. Saint Teresa of Avila wrote, "All concepts of God are like a jar we break, because only the infinite can contain our perfect love."

Take a small piece of paper and write or draw the image of God that is most meaningful to you. As you talk about these images in your group, put the slips of paper into the glass jar.

DEEPENING

The African American song "Run Home" has been performed by many contemporary artists. In the chorus we hear, "Go tell that long-tongued liar, go tell that midnight rider, tell the gambler, rambler, back-biter, tell 'em God Almighty gonna cut 'em down." Presumably, this song brought comfort to slaves who were suffering. They could believe that sometime, somehow, God would judge the wicked for their evil actions. Justice would be served.

In Amos, God is clearly capable of punishment on a grand scale. In his pronouncements, Amos makes it clear that nobody will escape God's judgment.

I have talked to friends in Benin, West Africa, who have no problem with a picture of a God who is all-powerful, judging, and doles out punishment. One friend commented on the book of Amos, "Where there is justice, God is. Where there is injustice, God roars."

Would I be more ready to believe in a God who judges if I didn't see myself as the one who might be judged?

So I have to wonder: is my image of God a result of my privileged upbringing? Would I be more ready to believe in a God who judges if I didn't see myself as the one who might be judged? If I use this biblical text as a mirror, it's easy to see myself in Israel's sins, as the one in need of change.

We also run the risk of keeping God in a box when we view God as judging and vengeful in the Old Testament, and loving and sacrificial in the New Testament. We don't have to look far in the Old Testament to see examples of God's great love toward the Israelite people. The exodus from Egypt is God's great love story, and God reminds them of this love over and over again. Amos reminds the Israelites of that love, grace, and mercy in Amos 3:1.

The New Testament also includes examples of judgment. In Matthew 25, the people are divided into two groups on judgment day: those who acted justly (sheep) and those who didn't (goats).

In North America, the pendulum seems to have swung from viewing God as a judge to viewing God as love. If we have been richly blessed, it may be easier to see God as loving than as an all-powerful judge.

Again and again, Amos reminds us that God is in charge. Perhaps we imagine that we are the ones in charge, and that we are blessed because of hard work and faithfulness. Perhaps these "jars" need cracking.

INTEGRATING

1 . On a sheet of easel paper, make a list of verbs that describe your image of God. Now make a list of verbs that describe the images of God portrayed in Amos. How do they compare?

2 . Do you come to the Bible for comfort or discomfort? Some passages can shake us out of our comfort zone. Who might be comforted or shaken by Amos's portrayal of God?

3 . Are there ways that you seek to control? How can you give control over to God? Some women live in situations where their lives are controlled. How could this image of a lion be helpful to women in these situations?

4 . Use charcoal and colored pencils to sketch images of God. Make a collage of the various images your group members draw. Do the images tend to be male or female or neither? How does your image of God affect how you see yourself?

CLOSING

Display the glass jar again. Write or draw one more image of God that has come out of your discussions. Put the papers in the jar and pass it around, with each woman taking two papers.

Use a spoon to tap the glass jar to symbolize breaking it. Each time the jar is tapped, read aloud an image of God. Allow pauses for silent reflection in between the jar taps.

Sing "God of Many Names" (*Hymnal: A Worship Book* #77).

Pray: *God of many names, you push us to expand the way we see you, and the way we see ourselves. Break the jars that contain you, God. Help us to see more of who you are. Amen.*

Four . . . .

Consuming Power of Women

READING: Amos 3:13-15; 4:1-3

OVERVIEW

Amos addresses the wealthy women in Israel, condemning them for oppressing the needy and poor among them. Their lifestyles of consumption directly impact others in the land.

As North American Christian women, are we in need of a prophet? Do we have consumption habits that need critiquing?

VISUAL: shopping bags

GATHERING

Lately I've been examining my shopping habits because my house needs to go on a diet. There is too much coming in, and not enough going out. Sometimes I shop because I really need something, but more often than not, I shop because it feels good. I try to justify many of my purchases by saying that I'm getting them secondhand at a thrift store. But the fact remains: I consume and I enjoy it.

In some areas, our family has tried to live with less. Instead of buying each new gadget that comes along, we are discerning with these purchases. While it may seem backward and irresponsible to some, we live quite well without a cell phone.

Many advertisements are aimed directly at women. Corporations know that women have buying power and influence over the household's spending. *Material World* by Peter Menzel quotes Charles C. Mann: "Because consumption occurs in the home, merchants direct their efforts at women whenever possible" (p. 10).

What conscious choices do you make as a woman who consumes? What goes into your shopping bags during an average week? What consumption patterns would you like to change?

DEEPENING

In this passage, Amos speaks directly to the noblewomen of Samaria, the most important city of the Northern Kingdom. They are called the "cows of Bashan," which doesn't sound flattering!

These women were sinning at arm's length through their lifestyles. They loved luxury, comfort, leisure, fashion, and feasting. But because of their desire to maintain a certain standard of living, the poor in the land were exploited. These women led costly lives—not just in the amount spent on food and possessions, but in the cost to human lives. Rich families were getting richer at the expense of the poor. They consumed at any cost.

Does this sound familiar? The North American consuming machine has an insatiable appetite. Other nations aspire to our standard of living, but consumption on a worldwide level at our rates would be a recipe for disaster. Each generation cannot have a higher standard of living than their parents did without having a devastating impact on the world's poor and on the earth.

Each generation cannot have a higher standard of living than their parents did without having a devastating impact on the world's poor and on the earth.

In Menzel's stunning photographic book of families from various countries, *Material World*, Charles C. Mann writes about the variety of people on earth, all with their own wants and needs: "It is foolish to imagine that they will not seek to fulfill [their wants and needs], surely immoral to try to block them from doing so. Yet satisfying their needs benignly will require enormous wisdom, if we are to keep people feeling whole, to treat all fairly, and to be graceful stewards of our natural environment" (p. 10).

We are interconnected in complex ways, and our choices matter. Society encourages us to always keep striving, to never be satisfied with what we have, to long for more. Our world is awash in a plethora of consumer goods and advertisements. Bigger is better; more is best. We desire the goods, we buy, and more is manufactured all the time.

INTEGRATING

1 . We lead privileged lives when we can make purchases to accommodate many of our wants and all of our needs. How do your choices impact neighbors around the world? What connections do you remember when making purchases? In what ways do we take advantage of the poor and needy without thinking of it?

2 . What does it mean to live with enough? Talk about ways to pare down your expectations of what is "normal."

3. Why did Amos speak only to the wealthy women in this passage? What unique conditions did wealthy women face then? What responsibilities do we as women hold in the church's witness? Maintaining our standard of living may mean that others are oppressed. When might we be the target of a call to justice and responsibility?

4. Christmas celebrations cause consumption and waste of epic proportions in North America. Do you have alternative family traditions that consume and waste less? Visit www.buynothingchristmas.org or www.adventconspiracy.org for creative ideas for reducing consumption at Christmas.

5. What does it mean to be a conscious consumer? Stores that support fair trade and fair wages for workers in the developing world can make shopping feel like participating in an act of justice. Perhaps this is our power as consumers—to choose wisely and give life wherever possible. What small steps could your group take to become more aware of these connections?

6. There are many great ideas in the 30th anniversary edition of *Living More With Less* by Doris Janzen Longacre (Herald Press, 2010). Consider reading this book together.

CLOSING

Sing together "You Are All We Have" (*Sing the Journey* #29) or "In the Morning When I Rise" (*Sing the Journey* #45).

Pray this prayer, written by a seven-year-old boy, Ben Zimmerly Jantzi, and published by Mennonite Central Committee in *Trek: a World of Enough*:

God, please help the poor get rich and the rich get poor so they know what it feels like. And then, God, let everyone switch back to medium and let everyone have the same amount of food and money. Amen.

Five . . . .

Justice in the Gate

READING: Amos 5:10-15

OVERVIEW

Amos refers several times to justice "in the gate." He may have been speaking his message from the city gate. The gate was the most public arena of Israelite life, where judges made decisions and where they welcomed the army. Justice was served here—in the wide open, in front of onlookers and passersby. What happened in the gate was a testimony of who the Israelites were, and who God was. Protecting the powerless and promoting just living was a key aspect of the Israelites' covenant with Yahweh.

VISUAL: tablecloth, dinner plate, silverware

GATHERING

The table is where many of us gather as families. Dinnertime is one of my favorite times of the day—a time to debrief and share about our days, and to connect while sharing in the nourishment that food provides.

Love and justice are doled out at the hearth or around the kitchen table. There are many times when we gather to

discuss, argue, or even pronounce consequences on a wrong-
doer. This discipline stems from our loving relationships and
our expectation that each person lives up to certain household rules.

The gate was where justice was served in Israel. Where are
the "gates" in your home, your church, and your community?

DEEPENING

In Amos 4:1-3, we can see the indirect injustice of an extravagant lifestyle. The Israelites are being held accountable for
their sins, both known and unknown to them. Israel has
interpreted laws to favor the rich at the expense of the poor.
The tables of the rich are laden with plenty of food, while the
poor in the gate are sold for less than a pair of sandals.

Justice in these passages assumes a moral obligation to take
care of the widow, orphan, escaped slaves, and resident aliens.
Amos calls Israel to remember the covenant with Yahweh
that includes this responsibility to the poor. There is a connection between the food and riches in a home and the treat-
ment of the poor in the community.

In our world today, many poor are still sold for less than a
pair of sandals. Girls and women continue to be sold through
the sex and slave trade. Children work as child soldiers and
are exploited for labor. In North America, migrant workers
live in appalling conditions and work long days for little pay.
Native groups live in substandard housing. Some of our cities hold countless homeless persons. Who is speaking up for
these people?

Sometimes I do justice at arm's length by giving to charities
and food banks. While this is good work, I wonder how I can

be involved more directly in justice-making. I can also do injustice at a distance by buying products that have been produced in intolerable settings or by not becoming aware of unethical ways that some companies use my financial investments.

Mother Teresa wrote . . ."Some people live and die in hunger. But in the West you have another kind of poverty: spiritual poverty. This is far worse."

Mother Teresa wrote, "There are different kinds of poverty in India. Some people live and die in hunger. But in the West you have another kind of poverty: spiritual poverty. This is far worse. People do not believe in God, do not pray, do not care for each other. You have the poverty of people who are dissatisfied with what you have, who do not know how to suffer, who give in to despair. The poverty of heart is often more difficult to relieve and to defeat."

Our tables should be set not just to feed ourselves, but to care for the vulnerable and the needy. It is often said that peace begins at home. How does justice start in your home?

INTEGRATING

1. What are ways that we contribute to injustice or evil at arm's length? How could we, like Amos, critique injustices done "in the gate"?

2. Many people in the developed world feel guilty when they think about poverty in other parts of the world. How do you engage in world issues? Do you tune them out, educate yourself, or act?

3. How do our nations care for the homeless, refugees, or undocumented people in our midst? What is the church's responsibility toward these people? There are many stories of churches providing sanctuary to needy people. How does your church act as a sanctuary and place of welcome?

4 . How active is your church in the "gate" of your community or your country? How does your church community serve justice to each other and to those in your neighborhood?

5 . How are your homes and churches places of welcome as well as justice? How does your church practice truth telling and accountability?

CLOSING

Sing "Come and Be Light for Our Eyes" (*Sing the Journey* #5).

Pray: *God of justice, come and be light for our eyes. We want to establish justice in our homes, around our kitchen tables, and in our cities and countries. Help us to work for justice in small ways every day, in the way we treat others and the earth. Help us to stand on the side of the powerless. In a world darkened by injustice, Christ be our light. Amen.*

Seek the Lord and Live

READING: Amos 5:4-7, 14-15

OVERVIEW

Amidst predictions of coming doom, Amos gives his audience a glimmer of hope. There may be a way to avoid God's judgment. If the Israelites seek God, they will live. If they establish justice in the gate, the Lord may be gracious to them. There is a chance.

God's purpose was not to bring destruction to the people, but to have Israel turn from evil to God's purposes. God's patience is nearing an end, but these verses suggest grace and mercy. Will the people of Israel heed this call? Will we?

VISUAL: magnifying glass or flashlight

GATHERING

Seek is a powerful word in these passages. In Hebrew, *seek* doesn't just mean "to look for," but is used when a worshiper enters God's presence to ask for guidance or instruction. When we seek God, we walk in God's ways and do God's will. We are fully submitted to God, active in God's mission.

When we seek something, we look carefully and closely, as if we're using a magnifying glass or flashlight. Our attention is focused, our eyesight keen, our senses heightened.

When we seek God, really looking for small miracles and signs of God's presence, it's surprising what we see. The things that we treasure, or focus on, can change us.

Open your senses to the guidance that God may have for you today. As a group, sing "Open My Ears, Open My Eyes" (*Sing the Story* #5).

DEEPENING

The only way for Israel to prevent the destruction that Amos foretells is to seek God and seek good. This is their only hope.

The word *seek* is used many times in the Bible. In Matthew 6:33, Jesus talks about searching for (seeking) God's kingdom before anything else. In Matthew 7:7-8, Jesus says: "Ask, and it will be given you; search, and you will find; knock, and the door will be opened for you. For everyone who asks receives, and everyone who searches finds, and for everyone who knocks, the door will be opened."

Amos condemns the Israelites for seeking Bethel. The Israelites worship God at Bethel, but Amos claims that they are not seeking God in their lives. Their actions show it. What does Bethel represent here?

Bethel, Gilgal, and Beersheba (see map on page 63) were prominent worship centers in Israel at the time. If the people of these cities were truly seeking God in their worship, they would heed God's call to promote just living.

When God's people promote justice, we seek to align ourselves with God's mission in the world. We are called to accept escaped slaves, resident aliens, widows, and orphans —the most powerless in society.

Listening to God's guidance can be tricky. Sometimes we may feel called to do something uncomfortable.

Listening to God's guidance can be tricky. Sometimes we may feel called to do something uncomfortable. As part of seeking God's ways, Amos calls the Israelites to return to God (4:6, 8-11). This term for repentance is used more than a thousand times in the Bible. It seems to be a common problem—the people need to turn back, over and over and over again.

How often are we standing in God's way, preventing something from happening? Are we intentionally walking in God's way, seeking life and justice for all?

INTEGRATING

1 . How do you seek God's will for your life? In what ways do you enter into God's presence to seek guidance and instruction? Share these with the group.

2 . How are you joining in God's activity? Where do you see God at work in your own life, church, and community? How are you seeking God's will as a congregation?

3 . We can seek God's presence on a day-to-day basis. What glimpses of God have you seen already today or this week? Magnify these by giving testimony and sharing them with the group.

4 . Practice seeking and listening to God. Sitting in silence as a group can be powerful. Light a candle and sit quietly for several minutes, focusing on the candle's flame. What is God whispering to you?

5 . Draw your faith journey as a timeline. Where did you seek God? At which points did God seem close? Where were the high points and the low points? Make symbols on your timeline to show these elements.

CLOSING

Sing "I Sought the Lord" (*Hymnal: A Worship Book* #506).

Share glimpses of your faith journeys. If you have made a time-line, share it with the group members, if you are comfortable.

Seek God in prayer as a group. Thank God for the glimpses of divinity that you have experienced this week.

Seven . . . .

True Worship

READING: Amos 5:21-23

OVERVIEW

In this passage, Amos warns against empty praise—the outward show of rituals, offerings, and music. God desires worship that is linked to justice. Our outward worship must incorporate our outward allegiance to God's ways by showing mercy to the poor and vulnerable.

VISUAL: candle, hymnal, worship symbols or artwork used in your congregation

GATHERING

We come to worship with different needs and different spiritual styles. Some people appreciate symbols and artwork, some crave silence, and some experience God through music. Worship is the outward expression of our love to God, and can also be a time when we experience God's love for us.

Some of my most memorable, moving worship experiences have been away from my local congregation—on retreat, at a monastery, or at a conference.

Think about a memorable worship experience. When are you able to give your whole self to God in worship? What moves your spirit—music, words, rituals, silence? Take time to share your thoughts with the group.

What concrete objects help you to enter into worship? Share some of the visual symbols or artwork that you have brought today.

DEEPENING

The Israelites were following God's instructions, to a point. The worship elements were all present: animal sacrifice, instruments, the singing of hymns. But they had forgotten what was truly pleasing to God—to extend compassion and care to the most needy. Arthur Paul Boers writes in *On Earth as in Heaven*, "Injustice and worship could not coexist in Israel's faith. Religion that coexists peacefully with injustice is false faith, deception, and idolatry. God's priority of justice determines the righteousness, or 'rightness,' of rituals" (p. 63).

Ideally, worship and justice should feed each other and be inseparable. A song called "Listen Up, People" by Bryan Moyer Suderman is based on this passage in Amos. He sings, "Listen up people all over the land, worship and justice go hand in hand."

Some people think worship is an individual act. But overwhelmingly, worship in the Bible is communal. In *Music in Worship: A Mennonite Perspective*, John Rempel writes, "Christian worship is corporate in its very essence . . . worship happens in many settings—in the serenity of a lakeside at dawn, in the fervor of a peace rally, in the intensity of a concert performance—but it is grounded in the weekly gathering of the church on the Lord's day" (p. 32).

It is interesting to look at the history surrounding the worship sites critiqued in the book of Amos. In 922 BCE, there had been a split between the Northern and Southern Kingdoms of Israel. King Jeroboam of the Northern Kingdom set up worship sites in Bethel and Dan. This was strategic, so his people wouldn't go to Jerusalem, in the Southern Kingdom, to worship. Jeroboam wanted the money and allegiance to stay in the Northern Kingdom. In 722 BCE, the Northern Kingdom was conquered by the Assyrians. It is thought that Amos preached to the Northern Kingdom around 770 BCE.

If I compare this timeline to my home church, it gives me pause. Our church has worshiped together in our village since 1840—about 170 years. Amos preached to Israel about 150 years after the worship sites were set up in Bethel and Dan. How would I feel if a prophet came to my congregation and told us we were doing it all wrong? Would we be seen as pursuing justice, or just gathering to lift empty, noisy hymns to God?

How would I feel if a prophet came to my congregation and told us we were doing it all wrong?

The word *liturgy* is derived from two Greek words that mean "people of God" and "work." Our worship liturgy is about connecting our work to God's work, joining in God's mission for the world. One of the Hebrew meanings of the word *worship* is "to serve." How can we use our hands and our bodies to worship God during the week, after our corporate worship is over?

God cannot be fit neatly into one hour on a Sunday morning. Amos is calling here for a holistic faith. What we do in worship is reflected in our prayers and actions all week long. We gather to worship so that we can be scattered to serve.

INTEGRATING

1. Why do you gather with others to worship? What does your spirit do in worship?

2. How does your worship support your church's acts of justice? How does it inspire lives of justice and righteousness?

3. How are our lives "worship"?

4. What parts of your worship are "noise" and could be done away with? Are there ways that God is calling you to enliven your worship and make it connect more with everyday life and the needs of people "in the gate"?

5. Take a quiz about spiritual styles. Corinne Ware's book *Discover Your Spiritual Type* outlines four spiritual styles: theologian, charismatic, mystic, and crusader. There are also online resources about spiritual styles.

6. Compare this passage in Amos to Isaiah 1:10-17.

CLOSING

Sing a song of praise or worship:

"God is here among us" (*Hymnal: A Worship Book* #16)
"Praise with joy the world's Creator" (*Sing the Journey* #16)
"God of our strength" (*Hymnal: A Worship Book* #36)

Read *Hymnal: A Worship Book* #820 together as a closing psalm of praise.

Let Justice Roll Down

READING: Amos 5:24

OVERVIEW

Immediately after critiquing Israel's empty worship practices, Amos gives an energizing instruction: "Let justice roll down!" Amos's message here is that where justice flows like a river people can be in covenant with God.

VISUAL: balance scale or an image of Lady Justice

GATHERING

Recently I read *Farmer Boy* by Laura Ingalls Wilder to my two young girls. In the chapter titled "Surprise," the teacher brings justice through the use of a whip to some misbehaving boys in the classroom. It was interesting to hear my daughters' reactions to this chapter. One said, "Those boys deserved it. They killed another teacher!" The other wondered, "Why would the teacher be so mean? I feel sorry for those boys."

Harsh methods of discipline for children have fallen out of favor these days. At the same time, countries continue to practice imprisonment, torture, and the death penalty as punishments for adult wrongdoing and crime.

Amos calls us to public lives where justice and righteousness are ever-flowing and evident to all. A high calling indeed!

There are many ways to define justice, and many areas in our lives where justice is needed—from the home to economic and societal justice. In your experience, is justice like a scale? Are the scales weighted toward one person over another? How are women considered in issues of justice?

The image of Lady Justice symbolizes a common understanding in the West of how to determine justice. The blindfold over her eyes symbolizes impartiality, and the sword in her hand represents the swift execution of justice. The church seems to be called to a different image—perhaps a woman with eyes wide open, who is partial to the marginalized.

DEEPENING

Sometimes we imagine that societal justice is like a scale, balancing the information so that justice is served. But what if the scale were tipped intentionally? What if scales were tipped to prefer the poor?

Amos makes it clear that God is greatly concerned for the poor. God is angry when the Israelites forget their covenant calling: to be a light to the nations, to care for the poor, the widow, and the orphan.

In both the Old and New Testaments, we see examples of the poor being exalted and the rich being made low. The Sermon on the Plain in Luke 6:17-49 includes woes to the rich. And we're told in another parable that it is easier for a camel to pass through the eye of a needle than for a rich man to enter the kingdom of heaven. There are ways of explaining away these passages, but the moral remains: if you're rich, it is hard to be a Christian. It assumes great responsibility, as mentioned in session 2.

On a world scale, we can see that the balance is totally tipped to the rich, with 20 percent of the world's population controlling 80 percent of the world's resources. The inequality in our world is staggering. The "Occupy" movement and protests in the U.S. against Wall Street greed have pointed this out clearly.

When justice prevails, God is there. When justice is allowed to roll down like a river, a new world is possible.

Even today, fear, anxiety, and uncertainty about our economic futures dampen people's moral obligation to uphold truth and justice. We are scared, so we hunker down, look out for ourselves, and ignore the poor in our midst.

Women suffer from inequality around the world, including in our own countries. In the country of Myanmar, many women are vulnerable to rape or forced marriage to military men. Women's bodies are viewed as sexual objects. Countless women are tortured, raped, and outcasts in their society.

The church is called to respond to situations of injustice, to give voice to the voiceless, to stand up for those on the margins. When justice prevails, God is there. When justice is allowed to roll down like a river, a new world is possible.

INTEGRATING

1. How would you define justice and righteousness? In the Bible, the Hebrew word צֶדֶק (tzedek) is translated as "justice" 102 times and as "righteousness" 394 times. The Greek word δικαιοσ (dikaios) is translated as "justice"

38 times and as "righteousness" 135 times. Does it change our definition of justice if we think of righteousness as a synonym?

2. Do you sometimes feel that your efforts for justice are small? Take time to list the various involvements—big and small—in your group.

3. Watch a movie about an inspiring advocate for justice. Examples include: *Romero, Gandhi, When the Mountains Tremble* (about a Mayan woman named Rigoberta Menchu), *The Stoning of Soraya* M. (about an Iranian woman).

4. Encouraging acts of justice and right living in the home is a way of joining the ever-flowing stream. In what ways are you doing this?

5. There are many women around the world who are voiceless and living on the margins. How can we, as North American women, stand in solidarity with these women?

CLOSING

Picture yourself as part of a great movement for peace and justice. Imagine people from all over the world merging together their small actions. As drops of water join to become a mighty river, think about the global church raising voices against injustice. Pour a pitcher of water into a glass bowl as you reflect quietly as a group.

Sing "Let Justice Roll Like a River" (*Sing the Story* #33) or "Let Justice Flow Like Streams" (*Sing the Journey* #65).

Pray: *God, you desire a world of justice and righteousness. As we join in this mighty river, we offer you our earnest praise and honest prayers. Please accept them as an offering to you. Amen.*

Nine . . . .

Complacency and Lavish Lifestyles

READING: Amos 6

OVERVIEW

Amos 6 describes the lifestyle of Israel at the time—one of opulence, self-indulgence, pride, security, and superiority. There is talk of extravagant lifestyles full of expensive perfumes, ornate furniture, elegant dining, and lavish entertaining.

God is judging the Israelites because of their pride and injustice toward the poor. The people have ascribed their successes to their own hard work—not to God's work through them —and have found pride in their military achievements. Most importantly, it seems as though Israel has forgotten its true calling, and this doesn't even sadden the people.

VISUAL: perfume bottle, fancy jewelry, ornate vase, or something lavish

GATHERING

Our family recently welcomed a refugee teenager from Afghanistan. Having her live with us has been wonderful in many ways. I have questioned my spending habits. I have taken notice of news stories from Afghanistan. I have learned more about Islam and her cultural traditions. And I have remembered that I was also a refugee.

Not I, exactly—but my ancestors were. They fled for safety, for a place where they could live and worship in peace. This is a story that is about 300 years old, but one that is still part of me. If I forget this story, then I may just forget to be mindful of the refugees in my midst today. My life is good. All of my needs are met, and more, sometimes in lavish ways. But I need to remember. I am called to remember.

This is similar to Israel in the time of Amos. God's saving actions, through the exodus from Egypt, had been forgotten. Life was good, and it seems that as the Israelites forgot their history, they also forgot their call to care for the vulnerable among them.

It is important to remember who you are. In the Jewish celebration of the Seder meal, participants tell the Exodus story as if they were actually there. What rituals do you use to help your family remember who you are, who God is, and where you've come from? Do you consciously place your trust in God, or do your possessions cause you to forget God?

DEEPENING

Amos accused both Israel (Samaria) and Judah (Zion) of being complacent. The *New Oxford American Dictionary* defines complacency as "a feeling of smug or uncritical satisfaction with oneself or one's achievements." There seems to be a fine line between being content and being complacent. Complacency implies self-satisfaction rather than satisfaction in God.

Amos 6 begins with a warning of coming death and destruction. In the New Revised Standard Version of the Bible, verse 1 starts with the word "alas." The King James Version begins verse 1 with the word "woe," which carries much more ominous overtones. This word was used to predict death or coming calamity.

There seems to be a fine line between being content and being complacent. Complacency implies self-satisfaction rather than satisfaction in God.

The people in Amos's time could have understood their time of peace and prosperity as a blessing from God. In contrast, Amos saw a selfish people who were blind to the injustices around them.

In 1995, I traveled with a group of Mennonite young adults from India, Indonesia, and North America. Our group was in North America for two months. Daniel was a sharp theology student from Java, Indonesia. After observing several worship services in Mennonite churches, Daniel spoke up. "I think that your highest priority in North America is comfort. And I think that it's the same in your churches too. You want to be comfortable. You're not forced to take a stand for anything. In Indonesia, Christians are. And it could mean life or death."

I've never forgotten those words. Am I used to a comfortable religion? Am I complacent in the way that I live as a Christian? When I read Amos's words, I receive an uncomfortable message. Amos's nine chapters are disconcerting, and possibly this is why many in North America avoid this book. We want to be comfortable and comforted.

INTEGRATING

1. What do these passages say to you about your lifestyle? Do our material possessions lessen our dependence on God?

2. In what ways are you complacent or at ease? How could you challenge yourself to be less so, or to act on the side of those who aren't at ease?

3. This passage refers to Joseph and Jacob. It is as if Amos is saying, "Remember where you came from. Remember who you are." What parts of your own story remind you to care for those less fortunate?

4. What are your dreams for yourself or your family? Do your dreams expand to include others outside the family?

5. Some say that the most comfortable church is a dying church. Many churches in Europe and North America have died a slow death and their doors are now closed. What would Amos say to these dying churches?

CLOSING

Sing "Longing for Light" (*Sing the Journey* #54).

Pray this prayer written by Dom Helder Camara, who served as an archbishop in Brazil from 1952 to 1964.

> *Come Lord.*
> *Do not smile and say you are already with us.*
> *Millions do not know you and to us who do, what is the*
> *   difference?*
> *What is the point of your presence if our lives do not alter?*
> *Change our lives, shatter our complacency.*
> *Make your word flesh of our flesh, blood of our blood and our*
> *   life's purpose.*
> *Take away the quietness of a clear conscience.*
> *Press us uncomfortably.*
> *For only thus that other peace is made, your peace.*

From *The Desert is Fertile* by Dom Helder Camara (p. 44). Copyright © 1974 by Orbis Books. Used by permission.

Ten . . . .

Turning Back

READING: Amos 7:1-6

OVERVIEW

Amos describes two visions of coming judgment to Israel: destructive locusts and a shower of fire. After each of these judgments, Amos cried out to God for mercy. His prayers were heard, and God relented from the punishment.

VISUAL: prayer shawl or special scarf

GATHERING

A meaningful tradition in our church is the giving of prayer shawls. We present them to 18-year-olds in our congregation as a prayer for the next stage in their journeys. We also give them to people going through hard times or embarking on new adventures. Women meet once a week to knit these shawls.

Our family was privileged to receive one of these shawls before leaving for a sabbatical in France. We packed our shawl, and I often wrapped it around myself for warmth. I imagined the prayers of our congregation following us and surrounding us during our time away, and this brought me great comfort.

In this passage, Amos earnestly prays for others. How do you intercede on others' behalf? Do you have objects or photographs that you use for prayer? Have you learned certain prayer traditions? Have you passed these traditions on to others in your family? Take time to talk about these questions with the group.

DEEPENING

A fascinating section of this passage is in verses 3 and 6, where God relents and turns away from the path of judgment.

God deeply cares for Israel and loves the people with a "tough love." God's decision to relent demonstrates compassion and mercy. Ultimately, the decision regarding Israel's punishment lies in God's hands. Amos 7:8 reads that God would spare Israel no longer.

The Hebrew word that is translated as "relent" can also be translated as "return," "turn back," or "repent." It is a word charged with emotion. Many of our worship services include a time of confession and encouragement to turn toward God and away from wrongdoing. We examine our lives and discern what changes are needed.

Does your image of God include a God who occasionally needs to repent and turn back? Perhaps, as in session 3, this is another time when we need to break our jars that seek to contain God.

Amos takes on a different role in this passage. Up until now, he has been pronouncing a message of judgment on the nations and on Israel in particular. Here, he switches roles and acts as advocate for the Israelite people. Amos bursts out a prayer of intercession for the people of Israel. He appeals to

God based on his concern for the poor. Amos begs God to forgive Israel. These prayers demonstrate Amos's compassion and desire for the Israelites to turn back to God.

Amos begs God to forgive Israel. These prayers demonstrate Amos's compassion and desire for the Israelites to turn back to God.

How do we view prayer? As something that will change God, change the world, or change us? Edward Willis writes in Guenther's *Hosea & Amos* of the Believer's Church Bible Commentary series, "Prayer does not change things. Prayer changes people who change things . . . Prayer affects a change of heart in the Christian community" (p. 333).

Jesus instructed his followers to intercede on behalf of their persecutors in Matthew 5:44: "But I say to you, love your enemies and pray for those who persecute you, so that you may be children of your Father in heaven; for he makes his sun rise on the evil and on the good, and sends rain on the righteous and on the unrighteous."

INTEGRATING

1. We can find other examples of God relenting in Genesis 6:6-7, Exodus 32:14, 2 Samuel 24:16, and Jonah 3:10. Take time to look up these passages. Why does God relent? What causes the change of perspective?

2. Take some time as a group to pray for others in your community, or issues that are affecting those in your group.

3. Amos engages in intercessory prayer regarding the coming judgments. Make a list of people and places for whom your group can pray today.

4 . Do you have a prayer rhythm in your everyday life? Are there reminders in your home to pray? For a week, pray at specific times in the day: in the morning, at noon, and in the evening, for example. During the week, record the times where you were more aware of God's presence.

5 . Set up a prayer spot in your home, if you don't already have one. What objects, books, music, or artwork would facilitate your prayer?

CLOSING

Take out your prayer shawl or scarf again. Wrap the shawl around each woman, one at a time, taking time to pray for each one.

Think of people for whom you can plead to God with prayers of intercession. Remember these people as you sing "Oh, Lord Have Mercy" (*Sing the Journey #47*).

Pray: *God, we bring to you our prayers of intercession.*

> (Pause for a time of silence.)

> *Meet us today, God, and remind us to pray without ceasing. Amen.*

Eleven . . . .

Feasting for All

READING: Amos 8

OVERVIEW

Amos describes another vision—a basket of ripened summer fruit. As opposed to the first two judgments mentioned in Amos 7, God does not relent from this punishment. There is a finality to this judgment that describes the end of the harvest, and the end of Israel through death and destruction at God's hand.

The wealthy addressed in this passage are far from God's ideal in terms of keeping covenant law. Food is sold in undersized baskets for a high price, people are bought like goods, and the people sell the sweepings of the wheat. They have desecrated the land, and lust for material goods has replaced their trust in God and commitment to the poor.

VISUAL: display of fruit

GATHERING

Summer fruit reminds us of abundance. The harvest, with all of its color and juicy flavor, is a wonderful time of eating and celebrating together. As many people return to the idea of eating locally grown produce, we rejoice with the farmers when the food in season is plentiful. We mourn when crops fail because of drought or other natural disasters. Feasting in this way connects us to the people who grow our food and to the land where our food grows. Ultimately, it connects us to God, who is the source of all life.

When I shop at a farmers' market or go to local farms to buy produce, I am more mindful of what I eat. I am connected. When I buy from a large grocery store, I don't feel this same sense of connection. I feel disconnected from the producers, the land, and even from God.

Buying fair trade foods also makes me feel connected to people—to farmers and producers in other countries. I love a bargain just as much as the next person, but paying a higher price for produce that is either locally grown or fairly traded seems like a wise thing for me to do. This is one way where I know that my money makes a difference in the lives of farmers, both here and far away.

How do you feel connected to others through the food you eat? What are your regular food purchasing habits?

DEEPENING

In the time of Amos, many Israelites were living lives of comfort and abundance while ignoring the needs of the poor in their midst. Their tables were overflowing with good food.

We hear staggering statistics about the great divide between the rich and poor in the world today. About 225 of the world's most wealthy individuals possess the equivalent wealth of 2.5 billion. Inequality exists everywhere.

The prayer of Jabez, found in 1 Chronicles 4:10, has been wildly popular in America, along with the book written on this topic by Bruce Wilkinson. The idea behind this book is

When we do not share our prosperity with others, or when it comes at the cost of another's standard of living, is that God's blessing to us?

that as you pray for blessings, you are brought closer to God's heart for your life. God will bless you with gifts beyond your imagination.

While it is a beautiful prayer, it can be abused. People may think that a life of abundance means one that God has richly blessed. They may not consider how people or the earth were exploited in connection with their blessings. It is dangerous to look at the homeless, refugees, the poor in prison, or people living in our Native communities as those who have not yet been blessed. When we do not share our prosperity with others, or when it comes at the cost of another's standard of living, is that God's blessing to us? Perhaps it is simply a result of our world's economic system that favors rich countries over the poor.

The Israelite people in Amos's time could have interpreted their time of peace and prosperity as a blessing from God. In contrast, Amos saw the price that others were paying as a result of their lives of luxury. He saw the underbelly of their economic and justice system—a people only mindful of themselves, oblivious to the injustice in their midst.

I had the opportunity to worship at the Weston Priory in Vermont one Easter. During a memorable sunrise service, we shared in communion while singing, "When bread is on every table, all will know that Jesus is risen. Then the poor of the world will feast and their children will sing, 'Alleluia!'" This seems to be Amos's reminder too—to strive for a world of equal feasting for all.

Imagine the world as a more equitable place, where land, food, and resources are shared. Imagine a world where we hear the cries of the poor, and people take action to right the wrongs. This seems to be the world that Amos calls us to embrace.

INTEGRATING

1 . Read the Prayer of Jabez (1 Chronicles 4:10) and the Prayer of Agur (Proverbs 30:7-8). Have you at times identified with one over the other? How would it feel to pray both prayers regularly—for blessing and for contentment?

2 . I am not comfortable knowing that my lifestyle and my consumption hurt others in our global community. What actions could this discomfort lead me to take? Where are you called to investigate, learn more, and act on what you've learned?

3 . Do we see our riches as a blessing from God? What is your definition of "blessed"?

CLOSING

Sing "What Does the Lord Require of You?" (*Sing the Story* #54).

Pray the following prayer that combines 1 Chronicles 4:10 with Proverbs 30:7-8.

Bless us, God, with contentment. Give us neither poverty nor riches, but feed us with the food we need. Keep us from evil so that we will not cause pain to others in our world. May your hand be with us always. Amen.

Twelve . . . .

Naming the Hope

READING: Amos 9:11-15

OVERVIEW

In the final section of Amos, we hear that the destruction will not be total. Israel's special status as the chosen people of God will remain as a blessing for the remnant of people who escape God's punishment. Hope lies in this small group of people, sifted out as grain through a sieve.

This passage is one of restoration. Help is coming for the people who remain. The chosen people here also seem to refer to the Gentile nations: Edom is mentioned specifically. This is a radical claim. Could Gentiles also be called by the Lord's name?

We are left with a vision of abundance—gardens and vineyards overflowing with fruit and wine, cities rebuilt. A famine has turned to a feast!

VISUAL: seeds or flower bulb

GATHERING

Most of the book of Amos contains a sobering, even disturbing, message. The last half of the last chapter of Amos gives us a different message: there is hope. Even though there will be consequences for their neglect and wrongdoing, the people will rise again.

The seeds and bulbs planted in our gardens contain great possibilities. They have the potential to grow and reproduce, resulting in a harvest that can surpass our expectations.

As you pass a bulb or seed around, talk about ways that you see the church bringing hope.

DEEPENING

The phrases "on that day" (v. 11) and "the time is surely coming" (v. 13) are phrases that have appeared elsewhere in Amos. These refer to the day of the Lord, a coming day of God's judgment and salvation. Israel has been awaiting the day of the Lord—a day that they understand to be military victory over their enemies. Earlier in Amos it seemed that the Israelites had passed the point of no return; they were beyond salvation. But this passage speaks of the hope of restoration that can only come from God. Destruction comes from God; so does restoration. God is in control.

Do we think we're immune to God's judgment? Perhaps many Israelites thought they were.

The message of God's coming judgment may have been taken seriously by some Israelites, and others may have ignored it.

Do we think we're immune to God's judgment? Perhaps many Israelites thought they were. Amos came to remind them of who they were and that their prosperity must not blind them to the needs of others. As God's chosen people, they were called to compassionate action on the side of the poor and vulnerable. Their call to generously meet the needs of the poor is eloquently stated in Deuteronomy 15:7-11.

God has promised to be true to the covenant with God's chosen people. Our tasks as the church are to remain faithful to God's call, to join in God's activity in the world, to see places where God's reign could yet come, and to listen with compassion to the cries around us.

INTEGRATING

1 . It is striking that nine and a half chapters of Amos contain challenging messages and half a chapter has a comforting message filled with hope for the future. Think about sermons you have heard lately. What percentage of the sermon challenges and pushes people in uncomfortable ways? What percentage is filled with comfort and hope?

2 . Imagine someone delivering an Amos-like message in your congregation: "Turn back! Remember who you are! Remember who God is! Care for the poor! You're too greedy, comfortable, and complacent! How can you feast while others starve?" How would this sit with you? How would your community respond to someone who dares to speak out, criticize, or tell the truth? How does your church deal with difficult conversations?

3 . At its best, Scripture can be a source of transformation, changing individuals as well as groups. What messages from Amos have impacted you the most? How have you changed as a result? Actions might include things that you could do today, or things that might take more planning. In what ways can your group respond to Amos's call? Be creative!

4. Do people respond differently to male or female prophets? In what ways?

5. Search your heart to discover the challenging message God may be bringing to you today.

CLOSING

Sing one or more of these songs:

"God of the Bible" (*Sing the Journey* #8)
"In the bulb" (*Hymnal: A Worship Book* #614)
"Whatsoever you do" (*Sing the Story* #52)
"Beauty for brokenness" (*Sing the Story* #115)

Set a baking pan filled with sand in the middle of your group. Light one birthday or thin taper candle as a prayer for hope and stick it into the sand. Have each person light a candle from the first one. You may want to voice your prayers aloud as you place the candles in the sand.

You might also take seeds or bulbs home to plant as reminder that God gives us hope.

Pray: *God of hope, we confess the ways that we have been complacent in the past.* (Pause for a moment.) *Equip us to critique our society and to energize our community. Help us to see the small seeds of hope around us. Like gardeners, we want to nurture the life around us into growth for your kingdom. Amen.*

Joining the River of God's Justice

VISUAL FOCUS

Place a blue, flowing cloth like a river in the middle of your worship space. It could be flowing down from a table or just rippled across the floor. Set tea lights on either side of the "river," one light for each person in your group. The tea lights can rest on small aluminum tart tins. Place a candle lighter or matches nearby. You may also want to display the symbols from the previous sessions on a table as a reminder of your journey through the book of Amos.

Song:

"God, whose purpose is to kindle" (*Hymnal: A Worship Book #135*)

GATHERING

Leader: As we worship together, let's reflect on what we've learned from the prophet Amos.

Holy God,
Source of justice and righteousness,
You have formed the mountains,
You created the wind.
You make the morning light and the evening darkness.
Yahweh is your name.

Songs:

"O healing river" (*Hymnal: A Worship Book* #372)
"Joys are flowing like a river" (*Hymnal: A Worship Book* #301)

CONFESSING

Read Amos 5:21-24 from a different translation or paraphrase, such as *The Message*.

Leader: God, we confess that there are times when we are complacent, when we have turned away in silence instead of speaking up for justice.

For times when we have chosen comfort over engagement,

All: forgive us, God.

Leader: For times when we were silent,

All: forgive us, God.

Leader: For times when we were complacent,

All: forgive us, God.

Leader: For times when we have ignored the poor,

All: forgive us, God.

Leader: But let justice roll down.

Reader 1: Let justice roll down.

Reader 2: Let justice roll down.

Reader 3: Let justice roll down.

All: Let justice roll down like a mighty river and righteousness like an ever-flowing stream. Amen.

RESPONDING

Leader: *God, we bring you our burdens for justice in today's world. In our neighborhoods, in our countries, and in our world, may justice and righteousness roll down like a mighty river. Open our eyes and ears to see your work in the world. Help us to join in joyfully, working for justice around our own tables and in our city gates. Amen.*

Leader: Let's think about situations in our lives that are in need of God's care and healing. As we sing this song together, light a candle and place it near the river as a small prayer for justice and for God to break in.

Song:

"Come, bring your burdens to God" (*Sing the Story* #50)

Share together what small changes you might make today as a result of your study of Amos. What changes might take more thought and planning? What could your group dream of doing on the spectrum from awareness to action? How could you work to engage the world?

Read together:

Hymnal: A Worship Book #732, a prayer combining the Lord's Prayer with words from Amos 5:24

Pass out glasses of cool water. Drink the water together, imagining God's healing washing over you.

Songs:

"My soul cries out" (*Sing the Story* #124)
"Let justice flow like streams" (*Sing the Journey* #65)
"Let justice roll like a river" (*Sing the Story* #3)

CLOSING

Leader: Come to the river!

Reader 1: Come to God's healing river, where justice and righteousness flow freely.

Reader 2: Isaiah said, "Everyone who thirsts, come to the waters" (Isaiah 55:1a).

Reader 3: The psalmist wrote, "As a deer longs for flowing streams, so my soul longs for you, O God. My soul thirsts for God, for the living God" (Psalm 42:1-2a).

Reader 4: Jesus said to a woman at the well, "Everyone who drinks of this water will be thirsty again, but those who drink of the water that I will give them will never be thirsty. The water that I will give will become in them a spring of water gushing up to eternal life" (John 4:14).

Reader 5: John saw this revelation: "The one who was seated on the throne said, 'See, I am making all things new. I am the beginning and the end. To the thirsty I will give water as a gift from the spring of the water of life.'"

Leader: Come to the river. Come to be healed, inspired, nourished. Take this water for the healing of the nations. Make God's waters of justice flow in your homes, in your neighborhoods, in our world.

Leader: God, use our voices. Like Amos, help us to tell the stories that need to be told. Speak through us so that justice can roll down like a mighty river and righteousness like an ever-flowing stream.

Song:

"How can we be silent" (*Sing the Journey* #61)

Map of Northern and Southern Kingdoms at the time of Amos

About Mennonite Women Canada

"A Place to Belong"

Motto

As each has received a gift, employ it for one another, as good stewards of God's varied grace. —1 Peter 4:10

Mission statement

Mennonite Women Canada (MW Canada) encourages women to be personally reconciled and committed to Christ and seeks to call forth the variety of gifts given by the Holy Spirit to build the church of Jesus Christ.

We commit ourselves to:

- Promote spiritual growth through Bible study, prayer, other Christian disciplines, and fellowship.

- Discern and nurture women's gifts and skills for leadership and service in the local church, the community, and the world.

- Build relationships and networks for support, affirmation, discernment, witness, service, and celebration.

- Support and strengthen the mission outreach of **Mennonite Church Canada.**

We do this through:

- Annual meeting and workshop at Mennonite Church Canada Assembly

- Inter-provincial/regional organizations
- Newsletters
- Scholarships for theological study through **Spiritual Growth Assistance Fund**
- Financial help for young women interested in integrating faith into life through participation in **Radical Journey**, an initiative of Mennonite Church Canada and Mennonite Mission Network
- **Pennies & Prayer Inheritance Fund** (PPIF), a home for gifts made in honour/memory of loved ones
- Supporting women working in Mennonite Church Canada's ministries with funds from the PPIF
- Stories of **"Women Walking Together in Faith"** in *Canadian Mennonite*
- Publishing an annual Anabaptist Bible study guide with Mennonite Women USA
- A blogspot: www.mennowomencanada.blogspot.com

We as Mennonite Women Canada are striving to do God's will and work where we are to the best of our ability. You too can be a part!

For more information, visit the Mennonite Women Canada website at www.mennonitechurch.ca/mwc/.

Or write to:
Mennonite Women Canada
c/o Mennonite Church Canada
600 Shaftesbury Blvd.
Winnipeg, MB R3P 0M4

About Mennonite Women USA

Jesus said: "I am the vine. You are the branches." —John 15:5

Mission statement

Our mission at Mennonite Women USA is to empower women and women's groups as we nurture our life in Christ through studying the Bible, using our gifts, hearing each other, and engaging in mission and service.

In living our mission, Mennonite Women USA:

- Connects globally by funding scholarships for women worldwide for church leadership training through our **International Women's Fund**.

- Equips women for caring ministry through **Sister Care seminars**. Sister Care validates women's gifts of caring and equips them to respond more effectively and confidently to the needs of others in their lives and in the congregation.

- Resources women's groups across the United States through leadership training, an annual Anabaptist Bible study guide, and *timbrel* magazine. Sister Care seminars are hosted by area conference women.

- Speaks prophetically and shares stories of women of all ages and backgrounds through **timbrel magazine**, the publication of Mennonite Women USA. *timbrel* is published six times a year and invites women to be "in conversation together with God."

- Fosters relationships around the world through the **Sister-Link program**—emphasizing mutual giving and receiving and validating a wide variety of gifts. Sister-Links connect women through prayer, letter writing, sharing resources, and face-to-face visits.

- Co-sponsors **Women in Conversation retreats** every two years in the East and the Midwest—a time for spiritual nourishment, reflection with God, and warm fellowship with other women.

Vision statement

Mennonite Women USA invites women across generations, cultures, and places to share and honor our stories, care for each other, and express our prophetic voice boldly as we seek to follow Christ.

We'd love to tell you more about our ministry.

Learn more about Mennonite Women USA programs—and get a little lift in your day—by signing up for our free monthly e-letter, "A Postcard & a Prayer." Just send your name, address, and e-mail address to office@MennoniteWomenUSA.org.

You may also access our website for our latest news and stories: www.MennoniteWomenUSA.org.

Mennonite Women USA
718 Main St.
Newton, KS 67114-1819
316.281.4396 or 866.866.2872, ext. 34396
office@MennoniteWomenUSA.org

About the writer

Rebecca Seiling lives in Waterloo, Ontario, where she is a full-time mom and part-time writer. She is married to Derek Suderman. They have two daughters, Zoe and Eden.

Rebecca has worked extensively with children, from camp counseling, to pastoring youth, to teaching elementary and secondary students. Rebecca is a member of St. Jacobs Mennonite Church. She has been a Sunday school coordinator, playwright, and writer and editor for the *Gather 'Round* Sunday school curriculum. Rebecca has written two books for children: *Plant a Seed of Peace* and *Don't Be Afraid*, both published by Herald Press. She currently serves on Mennonite Church Canada's Christian Formation Council. Rebecca is keenly interested in faith formation and outdoor experiential education.

Rebecca enjoys traveling, trying new foods, and learning from others. At times, she can be heard boasting of her experiences walking Roman roads in Italy, scuba diving in Honduras, eating escargots in France, and meeting Mother Teresa in India.

Although she tends the family hearth, Rebecca calls herself "quite an untalented housekeeper." Some of her sewing projects have lasted more than the length of her marriage. She strives to live simply and shops at farmers' markets, thrift stores, and garage sales. Rebecca loves to swim in the ocean, wake up in a tent, sing around a fire, and canoe on a lake as smooth as glass. She blogs about family and finding faith in the everyday at hearthstrings.ca.